Life Lessons for Grandchildren

AL (GRANDPA) ROWE

WESTBOW
PRESS®
A DIVISION OF THOMAS NELSON
& ZONDERVAN

Scripture taken from the New King James Version. Copyright 1979, 1980,
1982 by Thomas Nelson, inc. Used by permission. All rights reserved.

Scripture taken from the King James Version of the Bible.

Scriptures taken from the Holy Bible, New International Version®, NIV®.
Copyright © 1973, 1978, 1984, 2011 by Biblica, Inc.™ Used by permission of
Zondervan. All rights reserved worldwide. www.zondervan.com The "NIV"
and "New International Version" are trademarks registered in the United
States Patent and Trademark Office by Biblica, Inc.™ All rights reserved.

WestBow Press books may be ordered through booksellers or by contacting:

WestBow Press
A Division of Thomas Nelson & Zondervan
1663 Liberty Drive
Bloomington, IN 47403
www.westbowpress.com
1 (866) 928-1240

ISBN: 978-1-5127-5799-6 (sc)
ISBN: 978-1-5127-5800-9 (e)

Library of Congress Control Number: 2016915907

Print information available on the last page.

WestBow Press rev. date: 09/21/2016

Contents

Dedication

To my grandchildren:
Aaron
Zachary
Bethany
Preston
Noelle
James
Joshua

And great grandson:
Arnold

And to all who follow.

Preface

Old men have traveled a crooked, bumpy road full of life's lessons, with a destination sometimes unforeseen, but always the same. Along the way they form opinions and reach conclusions based on their own unique experiences, and, as they near the end of their journey, they become more focused on the end result than on the process. They have put lessons learned into a neat little package that they convey to you in as few words as possible. Often these abbreviated conclusions sound outlandish and preposterous. It may not be apparent from their words that they have learned their lessons through careful observations, study, and long experience. Given any single topic, they often feel they have already talked about it, seen it, learned it, digested it. Many prefer not to go down that road again because it was hard enough the first time. They, like Solomon, have found "there is no new thing under the sun." To the world these men seem opinionated, stubborn, and know-it-all. A wise younger person will try patiently to draw them out to get the benefit of their experience.

I Am Your Grandfather

**"Children's children are a crown to the aged, and
parents are the pride of their children."**
Proverbs 17:6 (NIV)

I am writing this to all my grandchildren. I'm telling you these
things hoping they will help you in later life. These are things I
wish my grandfather had told me. I use adult language because
I want to be able to express myself fully, with the intention
of providing a heritage that you may want to share with your
grandchildren. If you have trouble understanding it, hopefully it
is only a lack of maturity and education, and not because I haven't
expressed myself fully and well. Read it over again and again, and
it will become more meaningful to you in later years.

Individually, we have a relationship that is unique between
us, but because we are separated by time and distance, it is hard
for us to get to know each other well. Be assured, no amount of
time and distance can change the fact that I am your Grandpa,
nor separate us from the love I have for each of you.

It's good for us to know we are eternally bound together in
God's image with bonds that are both worldly and spiritual. The
eternal bond in the world is accomplished by God's wonderful
creation of man in his image. Our genetic structure is passed
on from generation to generation. I am eternally connected to

1

all the children that follow me, and I am especially aware of my connection to you. It gives me great joy and pleasure to know that no matter where you go, nor how much time and distance separates us, you always carry a part of me with you. There's absolutely no way you can be rid of this connection (hopefully you will never want to be). It is my sincere hope that, as you journey through this marvelous adventure-filled life, you will be aware of me being in you with all my love.

The eternal spiritual bond is provided by believing Jesus is who he said he is. I will discuss the bond later, but first I want to proclaim what I'm sure you already believe. I know you've heard the story. All you need to do is to make the decision to believe it. Jesus claimed to be the Creator, Redeemer, and King of all there is—and he is all that. You can find all this information backed up in the Bible, especially the Gospel of John and Paul's letter to the Ephesians (especially chapters 1 and 2). When you make the decision to believe these things, you have become an eternal member of the kingdom of God. Your membership in the kingdom of God is confirmed and sealed by the gift of the Holy Spirit who will come and dwell with you and will be in you. If, for any reason, you are not sure of the presence of the Holy Spirit in your life, simply ask Jesus to reveal him to you and you will receive the baptism of the Holy Spirit (look it up—it's in the Book).

The Holy Spirit is the eternal spiritual bond by which I am now connected to my grandchildren. By the unifying power of the Holy Spirit we are connected, not only with our children and grandchildren, but also with the Body of Christ, which is the Church. "neither death nor life, nor angels nor principalities nor powers, nor things present nor things to come, nor height nor depth, nor any other created thing, shall be able to separate us from the love of God which is in Christ Jesus our Lord." Romans 8:38-39.

My connection with you is, no matter how we are separated by time and distance, we can never be separated from the love we have for each other because of the sacrifice of Jesus. I am constantly reminded by the Holy Spirit, which is the love of God in me, to be praying for your health and prosperity. Notice that I didn't say "occasionally" or "sometimes". I said "constantly". So, as you go about your schoolwork, job, and family-raising, you can always be sure that you are in my thoughts and prayers, and that we have a powerful connection through the Holy Spirit to know when and how we need to pray for each other.

If I should get to heaven before you do (Jesus might come any day now to take us with him all together), you can be assured that I am continuing in prayer for you even there, and that I am dispatching angels to protect you.

I love you all immensely, and I hope you have as much joy in reading this as I have had in writing it.

How I Got That Way

How I Met Jesus

I am an ambassador to the world from the kingdom of God in the name of Jesus of Nazareth, who is the Creator, Redeemer, and King of all that is. First, I will tell you the experience that made me an ambassador, then I will tell you how I arrived at that place.

In 1973, I was attending a Methodist church with a Sunday school teacher who was a born again Christian. During a discussion of prophets and prophesying, he recommended reading the book, *The Late Great Planet Earth*, by Hal Lindsey, which dealt with prophecy. I had already read the book, *Chariots of the Gods?*, by Erich Von Daniken. In this book, the author describes, for example, the experience of Ezekiel's vision of the wheels as being a visit from extraterrestrials. When I read that, I decided I preferred to believe Ezekiel had a true vision from God. Considering that book to be basically heresy, I was very interested in reading Hal Lindsey's material, which I supposed (correctly) would be written from the viewpoint of a godly person.

In his book, Hal Lindsey discussed the end time prophecies of tribulation and judgment in detail. He made the point that if you believe Jesus is who he said he is, you have nothing to fear from the tribulation or the judgment. This statement is confirmed in scripture in John 8:24 and its antithesis, John 5:24. As I was driving to work one day in April of 1973, I was thinking about what I had read, and thought to myself, "I do believe Jesus is who he said he is." At that instant I was flooded with peace, joy, and love which I recognized as new life from the Holy Spirit. I had just become a born again Christian.

By putting knowledge deep inside me (I have since learned that this is the gift of knowledge and the gift of faith), the Lord told me that he had chosen me from before he made heaven and earth; that he is the only one with authority to make that choice; that once he makes that decision, he doesn't change his mind; and that no one can influence him to change his mind. He told me (again, not verbally, but by putting knowledge deep inside me) that I was saved at age seven when I went forward to confess him and be baptized in the Baptist Church. During the many years since being born again, I have found the Lord to be faithful to all his promises, full of mercy, love, and grace, and always willing to hear and answer my prayers. I have become fully convinced that in addition to all the wonderful things he has done for me, he wishes to do these and more for all those who come to him believing.

My background and walk toward heaven:

I grew up in the potato capital of the world, Blackfoot, Idaho, where my first memories are of a two room house north of the fairgrounds. Loving parents spoiled me and took me to the First Baptist Church for Sunday school and worship every week. I was totally spoiled with the whole world revolving around me by the time my first brother, Doug, was born when I was six. When I turned seven, Mom suggested that if I believed in Jesus as my savior, I should go forward in the church and ask to be baptized, which was the custom for all good boys raised as Baptists in those days. I seriously considered whether I believed in Jesus or not, then decided I did believe, and that I should do as Mom suggested.

I expected my life to be changed into a life of conversation with God. I thought I should be hearing from God, like Ezekiel and Daniel and David and all the prophets did. I remember that I asked God many questions. I asked for help often, but never got any response. By the time I reached the age of fourteen, I had given up expecting to hear from God. I had decided, since he wasn't going to be doing anything in my life, there was no use for me to try to hear from him. I decided to live my life as well as I knew how given what I did know about God, to do right the best way I knew, and to try to be helpful to as many people as I could. During these formative years, Dad told Mom, within my hearing, that kids should be allowed to play as much as possible, because there would be plenty of years when they would have to work after they grew up.

I was so self-centered that I preferred playing alone. Being alone, I could do whatever came to mind without considering whether someone else might want to do something different. I was set free by the knowledge that if God wanted me to live, there was no power in heaven or earth that could kill me. If God wanted me dead, there was no power in heaven or earth that could save me. Understanding that God has full control of my life made me bold in all my undertakings. Even in boldness, though, I knew enough not to take foolish risks, because this would be tempting God. I grew up spending many hours alone in the Idaho wilds, hunting and fishing—still my favorite activities.

During my early college years, there were lots of discussions about whether there actually was a God. One of the philosophers we studied made the point that it is wiser to believe in God than not to believe in God. He reasoned that if you believe in God and follow his commands, then there is a chance that you made the right decision and you could be rewarded. If you decide to believe in God and it turns out there is no God (no eternal reward), then all it costs you is living a decent life. On the other hand, if you make the decision to live a life without God, and it turns out you made the wrong decision, then you lose any chance of reward. Again I chose, in accordance with my Baptist upbringing, to believe there is a God. After all, I had committed my life to him as a child, and nothing I studied made that appear to be the wrong decision.

I joined the Air Force at age twenty-one. Near the end of my enlistment, I met, and later married, a wonderful girl named Julie Johnson from Omaha, Nebraska. Sometime during our courtship, I explained to her that I was a Christian, and we should live our lives accordingly. This was another step of commitment to the faith. Our son, Alan, was born with serious medical problems when I was twenty-eight. Within a few months after Alan's birth, my brother Doug was killed in Viet Nam. I struggled with why there was so much misery and suffering in the world. I reached another milestone in my spiritual development when I decided that God was not the cause of these sorrows. Instead, it is sin in humankind that causes death, disease, and poverty. God has provided a way of life that we refuse to follow, therefore we suffer the consequences.

Our daughter, Lori, was born when I was thirty-two. By the time she was old enough to walk, Julie and I agreed that we should take our children to church and Sunday school and that we should attend church. Going to church would provide our children with the same kind of training that had led us into the Christian life (at least as much as we understood of it at that time). We joined the Methodist church near our home and attended Sunday school and worship services regularly. It was with the Lord's help, as I found out later, that I quit smoking. This made it possible for me to sit through Sunday school and church without needing a smoke break. Not suffering from this addiction allowed me to be focused on what was going on in church. This is the time that I met the Lord.

Remember this important revelation: he had chosen me from before he made heaven and earth to live with him forever in his kingdom; that he is the only one with authority to make that choice; that once he makes that decision, he doesn't change his mind; and that no one can influence him to change his mind. I was saved at age seven when I went forward to confess him before men and be baptized in the Baptist Church. I have found scripture to confirm every aspect of this revelation.

The Life Filled with Joy:

We cannot suppress the physical manifestation of the presence of the Holy Spirit in our lives. Everywhere we go, no matter what we do, we take God with us, for he is in us. His presence will be made manifest. It is why we were created. Even though we spoiled it by our sinful lives, when Jesus comes in to remake us, he remakes us in the image of God, just as he intended for us to be his image when he created us in the beginning. Whenever I tell of the wonderful work he has done in me, he manifests his presence in me with water running out of my eyes. He said that out of our bellies would flow rivers of living water—in me it overflows its banks and runs out of my eyes. He says in Isaiah 12:3, "Therefore with joy you will draw water From the wells of salvation."

Transplant

To the staff at UT Southwestern Medical Center, Heart, Lung and Vascular Clinic Center, Heart and Lung Transplant Program:

Following is the text of a letter I was asked, as a recipient, to write to the family that allowed their son or daughter to be the donor for my transplanted heart:

To Donor Family:

As a Christian, as soon as I was told I would become a heart transplant patient, I began to pray that whoever became the donor would be a Christian. I asked Jesus to be sure that he would take charge of all the decisions, and that whomever he chose would live forever with us in his kingdom. Thirty-two days after I was listed as a potential recipient, the decision came. I know that many potential recipients have waited several years and some outwait their hearts, so I know the Lord has his hand on our lives. All the discussions of rejection issues made me not only resolute to do all the doctors told me to do, but also to go before the Lord and tell him that if he would give me a heart, I would receive it and care for it as my own, without failing to acknowledge the magnificent sacrifice of the donor and his/her family.

Before transplant, my heart had dropped down to just over 10% function, and I would have to stop for a rest when walking from the bedroom to the living room. Once, in 2006, my heart stopped when I stooped over to pick up some ice my granddaughter had spilled and I had to be revived by my defibrillator implant. Now, three-and-a-half years after the transplant, I have been able to resume normal activities, including walking the dog, doing yard work, working out at the YMCA, playing ball with my grandson, camping, hunting, and fishing. I'm even taking banjo lessons. I rejoice with every breath and every recovered moment of living.

I know you have experienced a great loss in your lives, and I assure you that I join in your sorrow whenever I think of the source of my renewed energy. I pledge myself to you that I intend to live this renewal in joy tempered with sympathy for your loss, and to live my life in such a way that it will bring honor to the memory of your loved one.

Grateful Recipient

From my wife:

Dear Donor Family,

We wanted you to know how you are always in our thoughts and prayers. When my husband was placed on the transplant list it was with the hope of a new life for him. We knew it would be coupled with great sorrow for the donor family. We have prayed for your family for over three-and-a-half years now. We are so grateful to you for the gift. We pray that God has comforted you. Please know that my husband has taken care of his new heart and cherishes his new life every day. He received his new heart as his own and has never had any signs

of rejection. We will always be thankful for each new day. Your family was the first step in our miracle. God bless you.

Recipient Family

I knew when I was asked to write to our donor's family there was no way I could fully express my feelings on such a highly emotional (for me) subject. I thought about it and worked on it for several weeks before I finally came up with the above. Now, several weeks after I sent the letter, I have realized there is no mention of the work of the hundreds of dedicated, hard working hospital staff that make all this possible. Nor is there even any mention of the fact that the work continues even after the operation and recovery. This letter is to apologize for not making mention of you in my letter to the donor, and to thank you for your professionalism and dedication.

I am reminded of the story in the Bible of how Abraham sent his chief servant with ten camels loaded with good gifts on a long journey to his brother, Nahor, to get a wife for his son. The story is in the twenty-fourth chapter of the book of Genesis and takes up the whole chapter. It is a fundamental story in Judeo-Christian tradition. Nowhere in the story is the name of the servant mentioned. Many modern Christian teachers say this story is an allegory of the Holy Spirit, because of his faceless, yet faithful, service. Though nameless, he is now portrayed in the image of God. I do not suggest that you should think of yourselves in that way, but I, as recipient of your services, should, for sure, have given you a great deal more credit.

There is no way I can remember all the names of the many people who helped me so kindly and patiently. I deeply appreciate the fact that you (all) work long shifts, night and day, dedicating yourselves to the health and well-being of your patients. I know you can rejoice over every successful procedure, for you have richly enhanced the lives of many people. Please know that, even though I failed to mention you in my letter to the donor family, I often recognize your service and dedication when telling others about my heart transplant experience.

I suppose you must resign yourselves to being humble servants, always lacking the recognition you so richly deserve. Please remember that Jesus, the King, also provided himself a sacrifice for us, and that he does not fail to recognize your dedication and service. So, until you are more deservedly rewarded, please know that I, for one, appreciate and thank you.

The Bread of Life

Jesus made several statements to the effect that he is the bread that came down from heaven, or the bread of life. I think it helps our understanding of why he repeatedly referred to himself thus, to think about what is meant by his use of the word *bread*. It should be taken to mean the general term that includes all food-- something like the generalized meaning of the word *meat*, as it is often used in the Bible. In English, we could substitute the word *sustenance*, meaning whatever it takes to sustain, or support, life.

Have you considered that everything you eat either is or was a living being? That is, in order to keep your system fueled for daily activity, you must consume and decompose something that is or was alive. If you think about it long enough, you might start asking questions like: Is life transferred to you from a formerly living plant or animal? Is the life that plant or animal had destroyed or is it converted into life in you? When you eat something, does it give you more, or less, or the same amount of life than the life you took from it? If you must destroy something in order to get life from it, why don't you run out of food sources? And speaking of life, how much life is there? Has life truly been growing and multiplying as it seems, and as God commanded in the first chapter of Genesis? Where does that increasing amount of life come from?

I don't know the answers. I'm sure I don't even know all the questions. These are the kinds of things I call mysteries. They can only be answered, satisfactorily, by God himself. Sometimes he reveals some of his mysteries to us in accordance with Jeremiah 33:3: "Call to Me, and I will answer you, and show you great and mighty things, which you do not know." I can share a few things the Lord has revealed to me. As we read and study his word, prayerfully, he reveals himself through the Holy Spirit.

In your Bible study time, you should try to get some teaching on so-called types and shadows. I have only heard about it myself, but I think a study in those topics could generate some important spiritual growth. I have heard enough to know that, basically, they are teaching that the attributes of God are manifested in his creation. In keeping with that idea, remember what I have been impressed to talk about in all these papers—that God created the universe and all that is in it to manifest (or make a physical image of) his spiritual attributes. His reason for making this creation is that it is impossible to be as great and glorious, magnificent and powerful, as our God is, and have nothing to show for it.

On the sixth day of creation, God made mankind in his image, and told them to increase and multiply. *In his image* means we are a *type and shadow* of God. The very next thing he told them was, "I give you every seed-bearing plant on the face of the whole earth and every tree that has fruit with seed in it. They will be yours for food. And to all the beasts of the earth and all the birds of the air and all the creatures that move on the ground-- everything that has the breath of life in it--I give every green plant for food." Genesis 1:29-30 (NIV). God made eating so important to us that we have to eat three times (or more) every day. Is that because he wants us to acknowledge him all day long for his life-giving goodness? I don't know where in the Bible it says so, if it does, but I like to think that is why we say grace—to fellowship, acknowledge and praise him for his gracious goodness.

As far as is known from the Bible story, food for all creatures was vegetation until after the time of the flood. You should always accept the Bible story as the first source of truth. When science varies from the Bible story, it simply means that science has not progressed far enough to reveal the whole truth. God told Noah basically the same thing he told Adam, except he included all living creatures as sources of food. "The fear and dread of you will fall upon all the beasts of the earth and all the birds of the air, upon every creature that moves along the ground, and upon all the fish of the sea; they are given into your hands. Everything that lives and moves will be food for you. Just as I gave you the green plants, I now give you everything. But you must not eat meat that has its lifeblood still in it. And for your lifeblood I will surely demand an accounting. I will demand an accounting from every animal. And from each man, too, I will demand an accounting for the life of his fellow man. Whoever sheds the blood of man, by man shall his blood be shed; for in the image of God has God made man. As for you, be fruitful and increase in number; multiply on the earth and increase upon it." Genesis 9:2-7 (NIV). As I said, it's pretty much the same thing he told Adam, except to include every living creature as food. After Moses gave the Law, the Israelites had to take great care to be sure their food, especially meat, was prepared and eaten properly, and in accordance with the law.

When many people followed him after the feeding of the 5,000, Jesus lectured them because they came to him seeking the miracle of the bread. He told them they should seek the bread that comes from above, and that he is the bread that came down from heaven, or the bread of life (John 6:22-59). He said, "I am the living bread that came down from heaven. If anyone eats of this bread, he will live forever. This bread is my flesh, which I will give for the life of the world." John 6: 51 (NIV). At the time Jesus was saying these things (read John, chapters 5, 6, and 7), he had just fed the five thousand with five barley loaves and two little fish, and walked on the water. Pharisees were increasingly alarmed by his popularity, because of fear that the Roman government would step in to stop their religious activity, which would put an end to the way they were making their living. The Pharisees did not understand Jesus' teachings, so they proclaimed them to be heresy and punishable by death.

Jesus said, "I am the bread of life." John 6:35 (NIV). And, "Whoever eats my flesh and drinks my blood remains in me, and I in him. Just as the living Father sent me and I live because of the Father, so the one who feeds on me will live because of me. This is the bread that came down from heaven. Your forefathers ate manna and died, but he who feeds on this bread will live forever." John 6:56-58 (NIV). When saying this, he was telling them that, as with all food, if he were to become the bread of life, he would have to be killed. The Pharisees set out immediately to do just that. Later on, as the time of his death drew near, he was increasingly aware of the impending agony. As he was telling his disciples about the end of the age, he said, "Two women will be grinding grain together; one will be taken and the other left". Luke 17:35 (NIV). The disciples asked where she would be taken: "He replied, 'Where there is a dead body, there the vultures will gather.'" Luke 17:37 (NIV).

He was telling the disciples that the woman would be taken to be with him. The knowledge of his impending trial was so heavy that this terrible vision of the vultures weighed on his mind. He knew this is why he had come, and this is what he must do. At the last supper, he told the disciples after he had broken the bread, "This is my body given for you; do this in remembrance of me."

Luke 22:19 (NIV). He was about to become the bread that would be eaten to provide eternal life to all those who believed him. In our Holy Communion services at church we still eat that bread as a sign of our belief, in remembrance of the sacrifice Jesus made to give us life.

Tithing

I first learned about tithing in the mid-seventies, when I met the Lord. I had been reading a book by a famous Christian author who was teaching that the Christian husband should be exercising a leadership role in the family unit. To fulfill this role, he should be going into the world to make a living and managing the finances, especially ensuring that the tithes are paid. At the time, I was working for the government and getting paid twice monthly. Typically, the first payday of the month I would have enough to pay the minimum credit card balances and whatever bills were due. Then I had to try to stretch the rest for groceries and spending until the next payday. Occasionally, one or another of the bills that were due would have to wait until the next payday, sometimes not getting paid until after the due date. The next payday I would catch up on arears, pay remaining bills and credit card minimums, and usually have some left over for groceries and spending. This mode kept me entrapped with credit card debt, and living vicariously from one payday to the next.

According to the Christian author, God's design for a family was for a husband's priorities to be: first, obligations to the Lord (the tithe); second, obligations to the family (sustenance, shelter, well-being); third, obligations to the Church (service, offerings); fourth, obligations to the husband himself; and last, obligations to the community at large (service, offerings). I decided to go with the plan. The tithe is ten percent, so I decided I would give ten percent of my gross pay and round up to the next whole dollar. That way I would be sure I was always giving a little extra. I reasoned that if you will be generous with the Lord, he will surely be generous with you.

As I recall, the first payday I tithed happened to be the second payday of the month, and when I told my plan to Julie (Grandma Rowe to you), she was panic-stricken. She knew we couldn't possibly pay tithe and all the bills and have money left over to buy groceries. I must admit that I agreed with her, but I was determined to enter the walk of faith, and to trust the Lord for his provision. This was a very scary concept, since it meant we would have ten percent less funds to pay the bills when we were barely scraping by anyway. I made up my mind that from then on I would live in obedience to the Lord to the best of my ability. This decision has resulted in unfailing blessings for us.

Part of the plan was to pay the tithe and all debts first, so that's what I did. Sure enough, we had three or four dollars left over after everything was paid. After seeing the result, Grandma, in an I-told-you-so huff, marched straight into the kitchen to show me we were going to starve to death. When she opened the refrigerator freezer door, we found enough meat on hand to last the two weeks, which, with the staple and canned goods we had on hand, was plenty to make it for the two weeks until the next payday. To this day, Grandma will tell you, positively, that the freezer compartment had been empty. From that day to this, I have always paid my tithe first, and I have never failed to pay all my bills, and we have always had enough left over to share with others.

Pay your tithe to the Lord. Immediately upon receiving increase in any form, rejoice before the Lord, thanking him for his goodness and mercy. Then calculate your tithe. The normal tithe is ten percent. There are some special occasions when less than ten percent is paid in the Bible history, but most of those situations don't apply to our way of life in modern times. If you pay ten percent, you know you will be maximizing your blessing.

You *are* paying a tithe. It's the law. You are paying your tithe either to the Lord or to the devil. When you pay your tithe to the Lord, you reap the Lord's reward; when you pay your tithe to the devil, you reap the devil's reward. The famous scripture of Malachi 3:10 says God will "open for you the windows of heaven And pour out for you such blessing that there will not be room enough to receive it." Why would you want to miss out on such a blessing? On the other hand, he says of those who fail to tithe, "You are cursed with a curse, For you have robbed Me". Malachi 3:9.

Paying your tithe to the Lord instead of to the devil is accomplished by bringing the first fruits into the house of the Lord. First fruits, in the case of those of us who are wage earners, means ten percent of our gross salary. I often hear the excuse, "I can't afford to tithe because I never have enough money even to pay my bills." That's because, if you're not tithing to the Lord, you are paying your tithe to the devil and reaping the devil's reward. Make your tithing calculation before taxes and debts. If you calculate the tithe after taxes, you are paying tithe to the devil first, for the institutions of the world are in the devil's domain, and your first fruits are going to the government.

Pay your tithe to the general fund of the church in which you are a member. If you are not a member of any church, join one (as the Lord leads, but preferably one in which the pastors and members are ministering the gifts of the Holy Spirit). If you are between memberships, pay your tithe to the last church in which you were a member, or to another ministry, as the Lord leads. The tithe is for the support of the staff and operations of the church. If you wish to give more than the tithe, this is considered an offering and is totally discretionary, under the law. By grace, you need to be paying very close attention to the leading of the Holy Spirit.

For your wages/salary, calculate ten percent of the gross pay, then round up to the nearest whole dollar. For example, if you receive $735.48, pay $74 tithe. Doing this will ensure that you are always a little bit ahead of your minimum blessing. When you find a dollar bill lying in the street, give a dime. When you find a dime, give a penny. When you find a nickel or a penny, give the whole thing, or consider that you are far enough ahead on your tithe that you can consider it already paid. Don't worry about this being too legalistic. Tithing is all about the law. If you are following these guidelines, you are maximizing your legal benefits.

Keep in mind that you are no longer under the law, because the law, by grace, through faith, has been fulfilled for you. But your freedom comes because you have been redeemed (purchased) for a price. Now all you are and have belongs to the kingdom of God. The reality is when you pay tithing (the Lord's tithe), you are paying yourself. You are returning material goods taken from the worldly system into the kingdom of God, enabling him to bless it and multiply it back to you. That's the law.

I recently saw a bumper sticker that said, "Science: it works whether you believe in it or not." Because of this and other stickers on the car, I assumed it to be the statement of an atheist, who seemed to be implying that religion only works if you believe in it. I'm sure I don't understand all the implications of his bumper sticker, but it made me want to explain to him that God's laws work whether you believe in them or not. In fact, the laws of science are simply one facet of God's laws. If you are tithing in the right spirit (Holy Spirit), you are acknowledging and rejoicing in the knowledge that everything you are and have, you owe to the Lord.

Sharing

Did you ever wonder why people try to teach their children to share? Most adults don't even think about why they are trying to teach it. It's just something their parents did to them when they were growing up, and "we turned out all right, so let's teach it to our kids." Instead of struggling with our children to give up the toy of the moment as the *mode-d'-emploi* of teaching sharing, we may as well recognize that this is a concept a child cannot grasp until he or she reaches the age of about six or seven, or gets to know Jesus. Kids who know Jesus are already anxious to share everything. At any age, it is important to make sharing a Bible based teaching.

Sharing is an application of the concept of giving as it is presented in the Bible. Jesus said, "Give, and it will be given to you. A good measure, pressed down, shaken together and running over, will be poured into your lap." Luke 6:38 (NIV). As with everything from God, these truths apply in both the spiritual and worldly realms. The reason everything from God applies to both the spiritual and worldly realms is that God has created the world and everything in it to manifest the characteristics of his Holy Person. He is the great I Am, and the creation manifests his glory.

Giving and sharing are basically one concept. God has given everything in the creation for our use. In Genesis 1:28 (NIV), he says, "Be fruitful and increase in number; fill the earth and subdue it. Rule over the fish of the sea and the birds of the air and over every living creature that moves on the ground." After the fall of man (go ahead and read some more in Genesis to refresh your memory), it was not quite so easy, since Adam and Eve gave dominion over everything in the world to Satan. Now, the unsaved people of the world can only enjoy those things they can take away from Satan, and then only by the sweat of their brow.

Sharing results in multiplication. The phrase in Genesis translated "increase in number" in the New International Version, is translated "multiply" in the King James Version. One person can work hard enough to supply the needs of two to four others (or more). Those two to four others, since they have their needs met by number one, can work to provide for even more people—and so it grows. There is abundant food, clothing and shelter available to everyone through sharing.

In the days before modern conveniences and fast travel, the family was the primary unit of sharing. When a man and woman came together, in love, to start a family, they bought (or inherited, or homesteaded) land to have a farm. They shared the work of making a living from the land. As the children came and grew, they were expected to share in the work. In those days, it enhanced prosperity to have a large family. The more people there were to share the work, the more the farm could produce. There was always enough to help others. The produce from the farm could be sold (or given) to citizens of the community, who then would have an abundance that they, in turn, could share. Family ties were strong, because the family members depended on each other for prosperity.

With increased ease and speed of travel comes more and more separation and independence of family members. The pleasures of the world draw men and women apart. They are able to get what they want from the world without relying on each other to provide.

All this is the way of the world of fallen man. In this worldly view, the family unit used to provide a measure of care and nurture, and safety and fellowship, for each of the family members. These days, all the family members, even the children, go their separate ways into the arms of the institutions of Satan—the work places, the government-run schools, or no place in particular. With time on their hands, people's selfishness allows them to indulge in all the harmful Satan-inspired activities imaginable. Drugs, alcohol, gang violence, and crime are all part of the *too much time on my hands without proper inspiration and guidance so that I could make something to share with others* syndrome. Satan's institutions are all for self, and against sharing. The worldly view is increasingly alarming (do you ever watch the news on television?).

Not so in the spiritual realm. In the spiritual realm sharing must still begin with the family, for it is here that the love of God is being taught to our children by means of the indwelling of the Holy Spirit. Christians know to take their kids to Sunday school, where they can be taught about Jesus. Eventually, the children will gain enough knowledge to decide for themselves that Jesus is who he said he is (John 8:24). Holy Spirit unity comes from Jesus, first, in the family, then, because God is infinite and eternal, his unity and love grows and expands to include all of creation. The love of God is the source of the desire to share.

Jesus said we would be left in the world, but that we would not be part of it. In John 17:15 (NIV), he says, "My prayer is not that you take them out of the world but that you protect them from the evil one (meaning Satan and all his dominion in the world)." Since we know that all Jesus' prayers are heard and fulfilled instantly by God, the Father, we know that all the forces of evil in the world can have no power over us. We go forth into the world, as the unified Body of Christ, overcoming evil with good, and spreading the good news of eternal life through the shed blood of Jesus.

The spiritual unity we have in Christ is infinite and eternal. No amount of time and space can separate the members of the Body of Christ. *Contemporary* is the nearest word we have to describe our relationship with people like Daniel, Isaiah, David, Paul, Peter, and John. The problem with using this word is that it relates to time, but our relationship is eternal. Eternal means outside of time. Our relationship with all the saints is now. As God has said, "I AM WHO I AM" (Exodus 3:14 (NIV). We are included with him in the eternity of that statement. Be careful with this understanding, though, because it has led the proponents of some religions to pray to the saints. This should not be done. Jesus paid the ultimate price to make it possible for us to come directly to the Father. All our prayers and petitions should be brought before the Father in the name of his Son, Jesus.

For born-again, Spirit-filled Christians, sharing is automatic. With the person and goodness of God indwelling us (Holy Spirit), we cannot keep from expressing the peace, love and joy that is within us. All the spiritual attributes of God are manifested in his creation (the world). If you have ever seen me telling about my experiences with Jesus, you know that, in me, the physical manifestation of the joy of the Holy Spirit is water running out of my eyes. Isaiah 12:3 says, "Therefore with joy you will draw water From the wells of salvation." Galatians 5:22 (NIV) tells us that "the fruit of the Spirit is love, joy, peace, patience, kindness, goodness, faithfulness, gentleness, self-control." These attributes are contagious in the world. When we are good to someone, they have abundant goodness to share with others; when we are gentle with someone, they have abundant gentleness to pass on to someone else. This is true even when we share with unbelievers in the unbelieving world.

Because we are members of the Body of Christ through the unity of the Holy Spirit, no amount of time and space can separate us from each other. In the spiritual realm, sharing is done in love. We know that we have all things available to us from our Father, who owns "the cattle on a thousand hills." (Psalm 50:10). We are delivered from the curse so we can share all things without worrying about whether we will have enough left for ourselves.

The Vision

I will share a vision with you. You can only get the full joy and wonder of a vision by the inspiration of the Holy Spirit. You don't see a vision. You receive it by opening the eyes of your understanding as Paul prays in Ephesians 1:17-18: "that the God of our Lord Jesus Christ, the Father of glory, may give to you the spirit of wisdom and revelation in the knowledge of Him, the eyes of your understanding being enlightened; that you may know what is the hope of His calling, what are the riches of the glory of His inheritance in the saints". Understand that this is my vision, tailor-made for me. It won't fit you as well as it fits me. But, just like a tailor-made suit, you can wear it in a pinch—it just won't fit you as well as it fits the person for whom it was designed. Try it on. See how it fits, and ask the all-knowing tailor, Jesus, to alter it to fit you.

You may recognize this as an allegory. An allegory is defined as "the expression through symbolism of truths or generalizations about human experience". In the King James Version of the Bible they called it a parable; although, usually, a parable is a shorter story with fewer symbols and fewer words. Pray right now, in accord with Paul's prayer, "Lord, give us the spirit of wisdom and revelation, that we may have the eyes of our understanding opened to know the hope of his calling and the riches of the glory of his inheritance in the saints."

The vision is of a tree. It is very large. Its branches extend in every direction, as far as the eye can see. It has a huge trunk, sturdy and wide. You can see that there is an inscription on the trunk, but you are too far away to read it. You are amazed at the abundance of fruit on the branches. Every branch is so heavy laden with fruit that it bends almost to the ground. It is free and easy for the taking. All you have to do is reach out and take it.

The fruit has special qualities. It never falls to the ground. Whenever it is picked, it is immediately replaced by another exactly like it. After you've picked it, if you were to let go of it, instead of falling to the ground, it would immediately return to the exact spot on the branch from which you picked it. As you examine the fruit, you see that each one has an inscription—each fruit has a name! Look! Here's a fruit named Peace. Here is one named Faithfulness. And over here is one named Love. Look! Here's another one named Peace, but it doesn't look like the other one named Peace. In fact, you begin to see that many of the fruits have the same name, yet each one is different. Look! Here's one named Humility.

And here's Joy! That's one of my favorites. I gather as much of that as I can get. You may notice that I'm not eating this fruit. I merely receive it into my heart. The gesture I use is to pick it and then bring it to my heart. This gesture is not necessary for receiving the fruit, but I do it to help your faith. You can't eat this fruit. You can only receive it. You have to receive it by bringing it into your heart. Most people have to be taught how to receive it. Since the only qualified teacher is the Holy Spirit, many people see the fruit and marvel at it, but don't know how to receive it.

Look over here! Here's some more Joy. I love that so much, I often just stand here and receive it until it overflows out of my eyes. Here is a very large fruit named Righteousness. When you receive this fruit, it gets all over you like watermelon at a picnic.

Oh, oh! Look out for this one named Patience. See how scrawny and withered it looks. Before you can receive this fruit you have to pick it, and then hold it in your hand until it matures and ripens. Most people don't hold on to it long enough, and let go of it before it matures. When they do that, it just goes right back to the same place on the same branch. The next time they think of getting some, all they have to do is go back to the same place and pick it again. But then they have to start all over again, letting it mature and ripen. I probably don't go after this fruit as often as I should.

As you walk around enjoying the fruit, you draw closer to the base of the tree, and you are able to make out the inscription on the trunk. At the bottom you see, "The Tree of Life". As you move closer, you can finally make out at the top "Jesus". Then as you move closer, you can make out the entire inscription, "Jesus is the Tree of Life". The vision is done.

Now, remember what Jesus said in John 15:5-11, "I am the vine, you are the branches. He who abides in Me, and I in him, bears much fruit; for without Me you can do nothing. If anyone does not abide in Me, he is cast out as a branch and is withered; and they gather them and throw them into the fire, and they are burned. If you abide in Me, and My words abide in you, you will ask what you desire, and it shall be done for you. By this My Father is glorified, that you bear much fruit; so you will be My disciples. As the Father loved Me, I also have loved you; abide in My love. If you keep My commandments, you will abide in My love, just as I have kept My Father's commandments and abide in His love. These things I have spoken to you, that My joy may remain in you, and that your joy might be full."

In the vision, you, born-again, spirit-filled Christians, are the branches heavy laden with fruit. As you abide in him, you are bearing fruit. As you bear fruit, you are glorifying the Father. As you glorify the Father, you increase the joy that proceeds from his love. There's that joy again. The joy I love so much. The world can't give you joy. The world can only offer happiness. The world tries to sell happiness, and sometimes it can be bought, but always at considerable cost. As with all things worldly, happiness is eventually destroyed. But once you've tasted joy, you won't care anything more about happiness. Joy is as far above happiness as eternal life is above eternal death. Once you are born again, abiding in Jesus, and filled with his life and joy and peace, nothing of the world can hurt you.

Righteousness: a Fruit of the Spirit?

Is Righteousness a Fruit of the Spirit?

When I shared the vision of the Tree of Life, one of the fruits I named was Righteousness. I said when you receive it you get it all over you like watermelon at a picnic on a hot summer's day. More realistically, you receive it all over you like a garment. But what a garment! Isaiah 59:17 (NIV) says of Christ that "He put on righteousness as his breastplate". In Ephesians 6:14, Paul writes, "Stand therefore, having girded your waist with truth, having put on the breastplate of righteousness". Paul undoubtedly had been reading some in the book of Isaiah, besides knowing by his own experience the virtue and power of walking in righteousness.

But is it really a fruit of the Spirit? What is a fruit of the Spirit? I really like the discussion in *Cruden's Concordance*. It says, "The fruits of the Spirit are those gracious habits which the Holy Spirit of God produces in those in whom He dwells and works, with those acts which flow from them as naturally as the tree produces its fruit." To boil that down, the fruit of the Spirit is gracious habits and the acts which flow from them. James says faith without works is dead, and, by the same token, fruit that is not received does nothing for the world—habits and acts constitute fruit. Notice that the gracious habits are produced by the Holy Spirit of God. To me, that means the Holy Spirit produces the attributes of God in the person he is indwelling. Jesus says that in order to produce fruit we must abide in him: "Abide in Me, and I in you. As the branch cannot bear fruit of itself, unless it abides in the vine, neither can you, unless you abide in Me." John 15:4. The whole point of all this teaching is to encourage you to spend more time in the word, in prayer, and meditation and study, in order that you may have the joy of walking with Jesus.

Righteousness is not named in the list given in Galatians 5:22-23 (love, joy, peace, longsuffering, kindness, goodness, faithfulness, gentleness, self-control). But, in James, chapter 3 (v. 13-17), where the writer is discussing the source of wisdom, see how he mentions several of the fruits of the Spirit and then writes about the *fruit of righteousness* (verse 18). In verses 13-14: "Who is wise and understanding among you? Let him show by *good conduct* that his works are done in the *meekness* of wisdom." Verses 17-18: "But the wisdom that is from above is first pure, then *peace*able, *gentle*, willing to yield, full of *mercy and good fruits*, without partiality and without hypocrisy. Now the *fruit of righteousness* is sown in *peace* by those who make *peace*."

Paul mentions fruit of the Spirit again in Ephesians 5:8-9: "For you were once darkness, but now you are light in the Lord. Walk as children of light (for the fruit of the Spirit is in all *goodness, righteousness*, and truth), finding out what is acceptable to the Lord." He writes in Philippians 1:9-11, "And this I pray, that your love may abound still more and more in knowledge and all discernment, that you may approve the things that are excellent, that you may be sincere and without offense till the day of Christ, being filled with the *fruits of righteousness* which are by Jesus Christ, to the glory and praise of God." To me, this scripture implies that the fruit of the spirit which he enumerated in Galatians is presented in a lump sum under the name of righteousness. If we're thinking righteousness may not be a fruit of the Spirit because it isn't listed specifically in Galatians, surely we have seen that it travels in the same company with that list in other places in scripture.

What is Righteousness?

Again, I like what *Cruden's Concordance* says about righteousness: "[Righteousness is] that perfection of the divine nature [meaning the characteristics of God], whereby God is most just, and most holy in Himself, and in all His dealings with His creatures, and observes the strictest rules of rectitude and equity." Of course, that now leaves us with the question of what does it mean by rectitude and equity. Equity means treating all creatures equally in all courses of action, such as in Matthew 5:45: "He makes His sun rise on the evil and on the good, and sends rain on the just and on the unjust." Rectitude means being right all the time. My wife and others accuse me frequently of insisting (wrongly) that I think I am right all the time. My reply is that I expend much thought and work to try to be right, so when I am wrong, that means I have failed in some fairly serious efforts. I am seriously disappointed when I am proven wrong, and I'm reluctant to admit the possibility without complete proof. That attitude is extremely prevalent among husbands, and wives are quick to admit it. Of course, any human's attitude of being right all the time springs from the flesh. No one can be righteous in and of himself.

How to Become Righteous

Righteousness, like all the fruit of the Spirit, is conferred on mankind by the grace of God. It is received by the individual person through faith in Jesus and the sacrifice of his shed blood. In Genesis 15:6, it says of Abram, "And he believed in the Lord, and He accounted it to him for righteousness." In Romans

10:9-11, Paul writes, "that if you confess with your mouth the Lord Jesus and believe in your heart that God has raised Him from the dead, you will be saved. For with the heart one believes unto righteousness, and with the mouth confession is made unto salvation. For the scripture says, 'Whoever believes on Him will not be put to shame.'"

The Jews obtained righteousness by keeping the law, except they were unable to keep it, really. The righteousness obtained through the shed blood of animals was usually lost as soon as they left off with the exercise. That's just like us. We feel so righteous after a period of study, meditation, and prayer, then we go to our job and lose our focus on God, and the feeling goes away. With us, unlike the Jews with their law, the law is written on our hearts instead of scrolls, and we have the Holy Spirit dwelling in us to comfort and guide us. Our righteousness goes with us, very often without us realizing it. Then someone mentions how they don't understand how we can be so patient, so kind, so generous, and/or so joyful all the time, and we realize we may be abiding in him after all. They are seeing our habits and acts.

The Benefits of Being Righteous

You need to know that if you have the Holy Spirit dwelling in you, you can rest in the knowledge that you are manifesting the fruit of the Spirit through your habits and acts. Stop worrying about whether your works are good enough. Remember what I quoted from *Cruden's Concordance* earlier, "those acts which flow from [those in whom He dwells and works] as naturally as the tree produces its fruit."

You are not justified (made righteous) by your works. Paul writes in Galatians 2:16: "knowing that a man is not justified by the works of the law but by faith in Jesus Christ, even we have believed in Christ Jesus, that we might be justified by faith in Christ and not by the works of the law; for by the works of the law no flesh shall be justified." Start walking in the joy of knowing that Jesus loves you enough to keep you eternally without regard for anything you do or say. As you continue abiding in him, his righteousness in you will produce the habits and acts that are the fruit of the spirit.

Study the letter to the Colossians, but especially notice what Paul writes in Colossians 3:12-17: "Therefore, as the elect of God, holy and beloved, put on tender mercies, kindness, humility, meekness, longsuffering; bearing with one another, and forgiving one another, if anyone has a complaint against another; even as Christ forgave you, so you also must do. But above all these things put on love, which is the bond of perfection. And let the peace of God rule in your hearts, to which also you were called in one body; and be thankful. Let the word of Christ dwell in you richly in all wisdom, teaching and admonishing one another in psalms and hymns and spiritual songs, singing with grace in your hearts to the Lord. And whatever you do in word or deed, do all in the name of the Lord Jesus, giving thanks to God the Father through Him." Notice that he is listing the fruit of the Spirit here. Have joy, peace, and rest in this.

Marriage

Introduction

This is not about how to have a successful marriage. Just to get past that, I will say, and this is fundamental, there is no divorce in heaven. It is not lawful, according to God's law, in the world. Only by the imperfect laws of man can a divorce be ratified. When the Pharisees tested Jesus about divorce laws in Mark 10:5-9, Jesus answered, "Because of the hardness of your heart [Moses] wrote you this precept. But from the beginning of the creation, God 'made them male and female. For this reason a man shall leave his father and mother and be joined to his wife, and the two shall become one flesh'; so then they are no longer two, but one flesh. Therefore what God has joined together, let not man separate." When he says "the hardness of your heart," He is referring to humankind's sinful, selfish pride that is the basic cause for all divorce.

Some say that, in Matthew 5:32, Jesus is making an exception for the case of sexual immorality, for he says, "But I say to you [1] that whoever divorces his wife for any reason except sexual immorality causes her to commit adultery; and [2] whoever marries a woman who is divorced commits adultery." Neither of these statements shows that divorce is allowed. The second part is plain--whoever marries a divorced person is committing adultery.

The first part explains that divorce causes adultery, except in the case of sexual immorality, which is the case when adultery has already been committed. In this case, divorce is not the cause of the adultery. In both cases, the events involving divorce involve adultery.

When there is infidelity, then, by grace, there must be forgiveness, not divorce. Forgiveness is the example God has provided for us, for when we were unfaithful, by grace, he provided a way for us. For example, the whole life and work of the prophet Hosea was to show God's forgiveness to an adulterous nation, as in Hosea 1:10, "Yet the number of the children of Israel Shall be as the sand of the sea, Which cannot be measured or numbered, And it shall come to pass in the place where it was said to them, 'You are not my people,' There it shall be said to them, 'You are sons of the living God.'"

To overcome marital problems and to have a successful marriage, one must have received the grace and mercy of God with forgiveness. One must come to the understanding that the law has been fulfilled through the shed blood of Jesus Christ. Commitment to marriage and family is the (super)natural result of being committed to Christ.

I will not be teaching more about that in this study. Instead, I will be looking at marriage as the image of the relationship between God and his creation. In many circles the idea of being created in the image of God is being spoken of in terms of *types and shadows*. This is another way of saying *in the image of,* which I prefer because it seems simpler to me. This is all scriptural as in Colossians 2:16-17: "So let no one judge you in food or in drink, or regarding a festival or a new moon or sabbaths, which are a *shadow* of things to come, but the substance (body) is of Christ."

This material is presented, intentionally, from my own interpretation, evaluation, and experiences. I make no apologies for incompleteness or errors, and I welcome any criticism and discussion that might enhance the material. It is not intended that the material should be treated as doctrine or used for guidance. The purpose of the study is to stimulate thinking, not only about God's relationship with his creation, but also about the relationships among humans and our influence on his creation.

Marriage Basics

First, we will establish that marriage is an institution of the law, both in God's perfect law of creation, and in fallen humanity's inadequate replication of the law. Knowledge of the law is fundamental to understanding the concepts of marriage. As previously stated, the institution of marriage is the worldly image of God's relationship with his creation. Law is implemented in the world—grace is implemented in heaven. Knowing how the law and grace work together in God's kingdom is fundamental to understanding the marriage relationship as it is intended by God. The complementary nature of law and grace is the subject of another study, but the synopsis is: law is administered through bondage, fear, and death; grace is administered through freedom, peace, and life—law is for the world, grace is for heaven. Don't worry, if you are a Christian, you have overcome the world and have been translated into the kingdom of his dear Son (heaven). You now live by grace, not law. However, as Christians, you are still in the world but not part of the world (to understand this, you could study the book of John, verses 14-18 and the first couple of chapters of Ephesians for a couple of years). Now, we will consider only the basics of law and study in depth how the law is part of marriage, and that marriage is the worldly "image" of God's relationship with his creation.

God's law provides order, equality, and justice in the world. For example, except for the law of gravity, the entire creation would be in chaos (which, in fact, Genesis tells us was its status in the beginning). The law, in the process of providing order, equality, and justice, is administered through bondage, fear, and death. Bondage provides order by setting boundaries (don't go here, do go there, stop, slow, yield, don't touch this, don't eat that, etc.). Fear administers equality by teaching the consequences of breaking the law (if you eat that fruit you will surely die; if you kill a man, you may hang by the neck until you are dead; if you commit adultery, you will be stoned to death); and by establishing authorities to be the guardians of the law. In God's law, they are priests, lawyers (Pharisees), and judges (Sanhedrin). In the imperfect law of the world today they are armies, police, sheriff, constable, swat team, gun and badge. In God's perfect law, justice is provided by the death of the guilty party. In humanity's version of the law, we, who (all) are guilty, are not able to administer justice equally, because we would be condemning ourselves. We moderate the penalties to fit our own evaluation of the severity of the crime.

We can see that marriage is an institution of the law because it is implemented in accordance with the law. First, we set the boundaries of marriage when we swear oaths to each other that we will "love, honor and obey, until death do us part", and swear that we will dedicate our love only to our mate, forsaking all others. In the law that God wrote to the Israelites the prescribed penalty for violating these laws is death (adulterers were to be stoned). In humanity's law, the threat is that of a costly divorce, and in some cultures, ostracism. Prescribing penalties for breaking the law is intended to instill fear, which, when the law is properly enforced, provides equality. Justice is done when the penalty of the law (death) is fulfilled in response to breaking the law. Law, as it pertains to creation, and to the institution of marriage, came into being at the very beginning of creation.

The First Marriage

Genesis 1:1-2: "In the beginning God created the heavens and the earth. The earth was without form, and void; and darkness was on the face of the deep. And the Spirit of God was hovering over the face of the waters." The first boundary is between heaven and earth; this is the beginning of the law. The first guardian (Holy Spirit) of the law is introduced. The earth is being prepared; the Bridegroom is preparing a place for his bride.

Genesis 1:3-5: "Then God said, 'Let there be light'; and there was light. And God saw the light, that it was good; and God divided the light from the darkness. God called the light Day, and the darkness He called Night. So the evening and the morning were the first day." He pronounced the light good, but what about the darkness? If the darkness were good, then why would he create the light? In my opinion, the darkness, as part of his creation, is good, but the light is better. On the other hand, the darkness, being the absence of light, which is pronounced good, may represent the absence of God, therefore not good. My next opinion is that this requires more revelation. Dividing the light from the darkness is a new boundary. The law goes forth from God's mouth. God's word is perfect law. God's word is his commandment. "So shall My word be that goes forth from My mouth; It shall not return to Me void, But it shall accomplish what I please, and it shall prosper in the thing for which I sent it." (Isaiah 55:11) Where there is light, there is no darkness. Judgment is administered when he pronounces the work of the first day as good. The Bridegroom is still preparing a place for his bride. Preparation continues through the fifth day.

<u>Genesis 1:6-10:</u> "Then God said, 'Let there be a firmament (expanse) in the midst of the waters, and let it divide the waters from the waters.' Thus God made the firmament, and divided the waters which were under the firmament from the waters which were above the firmament; and it was so. And God called the firmament Heaven. So the evening and the morning were the second day. Then God said, 'Let the waters under the heaven be gathered together into one place, and let the dry land appear'; and it was so. And God called the dry land Earth; and the gathering together of the waters He called Seas. And God saw that it was good." The boundary is set for the waters. God continues to prepare a place and judges the work good.

<u>Genesis 1:11-13:</u> "Then God said, 'Let the earth bring forth grass, the herb that yields seed, and the fruit tree that yields fruit according to its kind, whose seed is in itself, on the earth'; and it was so. And the earth brought forth grass, the herb that yields seed according to its kind, and the tree that yields fruit, whose seed is in itself according to its kind. And God saw that it was good. So the evening and the morning were the third day." New boundaries are set ("according to its kind", not different each time). The land is bounded by water. Remember, boundaries are the foundation of the law, set to provide order. God is still providing a place for his bride, and the work is judged "good".

<u>Genesis1:14-19:</u> 'Then God said, 'Let there be lights in the firmament of the heavens to divide the day from the night; and let them be for signs and seasons, and for days and years; and let them be for lights in the firmament of the heavens to give light on the earth'; and it was so. Then God made two great lights: the greater light to rule the day, and the lesser light to rule the night. He made the stars also. God set them in the firmament of the heavens to give light on the earth, and to rule over the day and

over the night, and to divide the light from the darkness. And God saw that it was good. So the evening and the morning were the fourth day." Boundaries, providing order, are set, dividing the day from the night. The boundaries are seasons, days, and years. This scripture contains the first mention of dominion (rule), which implies law enforcement. Rulers are the keepers, protectors of the law (kings, police, armies). In this case, the sun is made ruler of the day, and moon and stars are made rulers of the night. The preparation for the bride on the fourth day is judged "good".

Genesis 1:20-23: "Then God said, 'Let the waters abound with an abundance of living creatures, and let birds fly above the earth across the face of the firmament of the heavens.' So God created great sea creatures and every living thing that moves, with which the waters abounded, according to their kind, and every winged bird according to its kind. And God saw that it was good. And God blessed them, saying, 'Be fruitful, and multiply, and fill the water in the seas, and let birds multiply on the earth.' So the evening and morning were the fifth day."

Genesis 1:24-31: "Then God said, 'Let the earth bring forth the living creature according to its kind: cattle and creeping thing and beast of the earth, each according to its kind'; and it was so. And God made the beast of the earth according to its kind, cattle according to its kind, and everything that creeps on the earth according to its kind. And God saw that it was good. Then God said, 'Let Us make man in Our image, according to Our likeness; let them have dominion over the fish of the sea, over the birds of the air, and over the cattle, over all the earth and over every creeping thing that creeps on the earth.' So God created man in His own image; in the image of God He created him; male and female He created them. Then God blessed them, and God said to them, 'Be fruitful and multiply; fill the earth and subdue it; have dominion over the fish of the sea, over the birds of the air, and over every living thing that moves on the earth.' And God said, 'See, I have given you every herb that yields seed, which is on the face of all the earth, and every tree whose fruit yields seed; to you it shall be for food. Also, to every beast of the earth, to every bird of the air, and to everything that creeps on the earth, in which there is life, I have given every green herb for food'; and it was so. Then God saw everything that He had made, and indeed it was very good. So the evening and the morning were the sixth day."

The sixth day! This is the glorious completion of God's wonderful, marvelous, infinite creation, his bride. The law is completed, the marriage is consummated, offspring with attributes of both God and Earth are formed. The law is perfected when he has completed the boundaries, given the signs in the heavens to provide guidance, provided the food necessary to carry out his commandment to multiply, and established man as the keeper of the law.

Notice in verse 24, he is not saying he created—rather that he commanded the earth to bring forth. I'm sure many theologians will disagree, but I believe when God said, "Let Us make man in Our image", he was continuing in commanding the earth in the creation process. For the special project at hand he was not limiting it to the earth to bring forth man "in Our image". In fact, his participation (Genesis 2:7: "And the Lord God formed man of the dust of the ground, and breathed into his nostrils the breath of life; and man became a living being.") is representative of the image of the consummation of a marriage. The image in the world that shows this heavenly relationship is when a man and woman come together in marriage and have babies that have the characteristics of both parents. The bringing forth of offspring with the characteristics of both God and his beloved Creation, completes the creation process to perfection and to his delight ("indeed it was very good.").

Here you should notice that the work at the end of the sixth day was not just good, but it was *very* good. It was perfect and wonderful and entitled to a "behold (KJV)"! He was looking at his work with great joy and pleasure and satisfaction. This is the same kind of feeling we feel when a plan comes together with perfect results. In fact, he was so pleased and satisfied that he took the whole next day off, to rest and enjoy his work. Do you have any idea what he might have done on the eighth day? It is a mystery. If you know, and tell me, I will know whether you have been with the Lord. Here is probably a good place to remind you that God did not *marry* the earth. Remember, this study is intended to show the institution of marriage in the world as the image of God's relationship with his creation.

The Second Marriage

Genesis 2:18, 21-24: "And the Lord God said, 'It is not good that man should be alone; I will make him a helper comparable to him'. (21) "And the Lord God caused a deep sleep to fall on Adam, and he slept; and He took one of his ribs, and closed up the flesh in it's place. Then the rib which the Lord God had taken from man He made into a woman, and He brought her to the man. And Adam said: 'This is now bone of my bones And flesh of my flesh; She shall be called Woman, Because she was taken out of Man.' Therefore a man shall leave his father and mother and be joined to his wife, and they shall become one flesh." Adam was well pleased with his helper. He immediately recognized the unity of the flesh. This unity continues throughout the generations through the passing on of the genetic material which all comes from the one man, Adam. This is the worldly image of God's creation containing all the characteristics of his own being, the great I AM. Man is created in God's image and given dominion over all that is created.

But Adam failed as a ruler. He failed to keep and protect the law. He didn't keep Eve from eating of the fruit of the Tree of Knowledge of Good and Evil, and then he ate it himself. Before they even consummated their marriage they divorced themselves from their reason for being. Not only could they not continue to rule over their kingdom themselves, but now they would be unable to pass the reins (or the reigns) on to their children. God had breathed into them the breath of life (his Spirit), and they had rejected their heavenly connection. Now they were returned to the dust from which they were formed. When they finally consummated their marriage, their first offspring continued in the law breaking mode by killing his brother. From that point on, matters only got worse.

The Bible tells us in Genesis 6:5-6: "Then the Lord saw that the wickedness of man was great in the earth, and that every intent of the thoughts of his heart was only evil continually. And the Lord was sorry that He had made man on the earth, and He was grieved in His heart." His wonderful creation was spoiled and he was grieved in his heart. How disappointing it is to see your work done so completely wonderfully that if you had done anything more it would have been less perfect, only to see it so completely ruined that it makes you feel bad that you had even started it. It was time to implement divorce proceedings. In verse 7 we read, "So the Lord said, 'I will destroy man whom I have created from the face of the earth, both man and beast, creeping thing and birds of the air, for I am sorry that I have made them.'"

Genesis 6:8: "But Noah found grace in the eyes of the Lord." Let us all thank God for Noah, because without him there wouldn't be any us. But more importantly, let us all thank God for grace. Remember that I said grace is in the heavenly kingdom, and law is in the worldly kingdom? Through grace, God is able to establish a plan for remaking his spoiled relationship. He will accomplish it by re-marrying (or un-divorcing) his creation. He begins the process by removing the curse from the ground, expanding the food supply (to include meat from animals), and renewing the commandment to multiply and replenish the earth.

The Third? (Final?) Marriage

Building toward the re-marriage is carried through from here until the Holy Spirit causes the Virgin Mary to become pregnant with the Son of God, the Son of Man, Jesus. With the birth of Jesus, the kingdom of God is reestablished upon the earth. The imagery is completed when we enter into the marriage supper of the Lamb in Revelation 19:7-11. The Church here is called the wife, which implies consummation has already taken place. I hold that this consummation happened at Pentecost, when the Holy Spirit was given to the Church. Each believer is consummated at the time he/she receives the Holy Spirit and is born again. It is then that the believer is made to "see the kingdom of God" (John 3:3). The marriage supper of the Lamb described in Revelation is the celebration of Christ having overcome all his enemies, and having prepared a heavenly home (the "New Jerusalem"), without sin or darkness, in the kingdom of God, into which to receive his wife. This imagery of marriage is used throughout the Bible to show the relationship of God with his creation.

The reason for the question marks after *Third* and *Final* in the section heading is to highlight my lack of revelation concerning several aspects of God's rebuilding and re-marrying processes. It seems likely to me, but not truly revealed, that there should be a total of at least six marriages, to parallel the six-day process of creation. Then after the sixth marriage, it would seem likely that perfection would be achieved, and the marriage supper of the Lamb would be equivalent to God's Sabbath—the day of rest and celebration of a work perfectly completed. So far, my revelation has not included these concepts. In any discussion of the kingdom of God and his relation to his creation, no single believer should claim to have a full understanding of the majesty and glory of God's kingdom.

We are mortal and finite in the world. God is eternal and infinite in all his characteristics. Possibly (maybe), when we are changed into our immortal forms we will understand all. I doubt it, but almost certainly we will understand more. What I have written here is what the Lord has shown me so far. Beyond that I can only speculate and ask questions. The most important thing to remember is that once you confess Jesus (Romans 10:10) you receive salvation, and when you believe in your heart that Jesus is who he said he is (Romans 10:10, John 8:24), you will receive the righteousness of Christ and be translated "into the kingdom of His dear Son." Colossians 1:13 (KJV). When, in accordance with John 3:3 (KJV) ("except a man be born again, he cannot see the kingdom of God."), you have been enabled to see the kingdom of God, you can avail yourself of the promise of Jeremiah 33:3, "Call to Me, and I will answer you, and show you great and mighty things, which you do not know."

Law and Grace

Summary

At the end of time, already seen in heaven, creation and heaven are one, and God, in Christ, is all in all, the Great I Am. Law and grace are all about Jesus. Everything that is, is all about Jesus. Jesus is the Alpha and Omega, the Beginning and the End, the First and the Last. Pertaining to law and grace, Jesus is the Lion and the Lamb. The lion is the symbol of law: dominion, power, and judgment; the lamb is the symbol of grace: humility, peace, and mercy. Throughout the ages, beginning with the institution of marriage, God has provided the imagery that foreshadows the fulfillment of his plan. Law and grace are complementary, and each is made perfect by the other. Law is given to provide order, equality, and justice. Grace is given to provide harmony, unity, and mercy. Law has dominion over creation. Grace has dominion over heaven. God's design, as revealed in the Bible, is the perfect union of law and grace into one domain where there is order with harmony, equality with unity, and justice with mercy.

Because of sin there is separation between the dominion of law and the dominion of grace. The manifestation of God's glory is perfected when all evil has been destroyed, and God, in Christ, has dominion over heaven and earth. He will be "all in all" (I Corinthians 15:28). In the kingdom of God the work is finished, but creation is passing through time until it reaches the fulfillment of God's plan. Most importantly, once we have believed God and received the Holy Spirit, we must learn to overcome the world, the flesh and the devil, and to live by grace, and not by the law. We are dead to the law but alive to grace through faith in Jesus. We can tell whether we are trying to live by the law if we are setting boundaries for ourselves, or if we are trying to live according to the boundaries set by others. If anyone is telling us that we must do this or that, and if we don't, we must pay a penalty (usually death), then we are being bound by the law. Living by grace means freedom (no boundaries), peace (no fear of death), and life (not death) eternal. By grace we can "do all things through Christ who strengthens (us)." (Philippians 4:13).

Introduction

Paul teaches in Romans 7:7-25 that we are born with a conscience, which causes us to struggle from time to time with the idea that we need to be leading better lives—that the lives we are leading are full of sin. In fact, we should study in Romans chapters 5-8 to get the full flavor of the trouble we are in without grace under the law. Notice, we are studying law *and* grace, not law *vs.* grace. It is not law fighting against grace. We cannot put aside the law and forget it, precisely because of the issues Paul describes in his letter. The law is perfect, but we are unable to keep it as long as we live our lives according to the law. What we struggle with is that by grace, through faith, the law is fulfilled. When we struggle against sin, it is faith that is lacking. Faith is knowledge of things not seen (the gift of God, given by the Holy Spirit). It is through faith that we live by grace. When we enter into the kingdom of God through faith in Jesus, we enter into a state of grace where the law is fulfilled and written on our hearts. In the kingdom of

God the law has been made perfect and complete and fulfilled by grace. The law is perfected by grace through the shed blood of Jesus, and grace is completed through the fulfillment of the law.

Law and Grace

We already studied about marriage being the image of God's relationship with his creation. He said in marriage the two should become one. Unity comes from the Holy Spirit. When God breathed his life (Holy Spirit) into the man he became a living being (the first marriage), creating the union (unity) between God and his creation. God gave dominion of the earth to man, and God was united with man, reigning over man from the kingdom of God, therefore, God, through mankind, had dominion over heaven and earth. But man wanted a divorce (speaking in the imagery of marriage). He broke away from the dominion of God to create his own kingdom. This separated man, the reigning entity over creation, from grace. In the kingdom of the world, the law can only be fulfilled by justice. In the creation, without grace, justice is without mercy, thus requiring the administration of death as the penalty for breaking the law. Death is symbolized, and caused by, the shedding of blood (life is in the blood [Genesis 9:4]).

But God doesn't do divorce (again speaking in the imagery of marriage). He still has the ultimate dominion, and his will prevails. His dominion includes grace. His grace is eternal, and is present in all his dealings with his creation throughout eternity. God administers grace (through faith) with mercy, by taking the punishment upon himself through the shed blood and death of his Son, Jesus of Nazareth. Because his death must occur at only one point in time, relative to the creation, God made promises to men of this coming redemption in the form of covenants.

The covenants of God are always sealed and confirmed by the shedding of blood, which is always foreshadowing the shed blood of Jesus.

The first shedding of blood occurred at the second marriage, when God took the rib from Adam to form Eve. The covenants are always given by the grace of God. That is, they are one-sided, the unmerited favor of God. He makes the promise to mankind, and provides the sacrifice to seal it in blood. In the same way, the propitiation for sin, according to the law, is the shedding of blood. Once the blood has been shed, it is offered, by faith, to God, who accepts it as the fulfillment of the requirement of the law. The shed blood seals the covenant given by grace. In temple worship, the shed blood of sheep and goats was brought into the presence of God and offered, in faith, as a sacrifice. God, accepted, by grace, the shed blood as the redemption from sin, according to the covenant (law) given to Moses.

Conclusion

God has continued his plan of redemption through the ages with covenants given through Noah, then Abraham, then Israel, then Moses, then David, and ultimately through Jesus, the Savior, Priest, King, Son of God and Son of Man. He created everything perfect in the beginning and now has provided the redemption needed for restoration. He has provided all we need to reclaim our right to dominion over creation. According to Hebrews 12:2, Jesus is the "author and finisher of our faith." He has provided the shed blood, required for fulfilling the law, and the faith, required for entering into grace. All that is left for us to do is to believe and receive.

Dominion

**"To God our Savior, Who alone is wise, Be glory
and majesty, Dominion and power, Both now and
forever. Amen."**

(Jude 25).

It has been observed that animals must change their behavior
to survive in their environment. They must migrate or hibernate
to survive the winter, for example. But mankind changes the
environment to fit their lifestyle. They build houses to live in, cars
and roads for traveling over the land, and bridges and boats for
travel over and on the water. This is according to God's command
in Genesis for man to have dominion. *Cruden's Concordance* says
dominion is "The universal and unlimited authority of God,"
referencing Psalm 72:8 and 145:13, Daniel 4:3, 22, 34, and 7:14.
All these references, except Daniel 4:22, are referencing the
ultimate dominion of God over heaven and earth (Daniel 4:22
refers to the reign of King Nebuchadnezzar).

The first use of the word *dominion* in the New King James
Version of the Bible is in Genesis 1:26, where God commands
creation: "Let Us make man in Our image, according to Our
likeness; let them have dominion over the fish of the sea, over
the birds of the air, and over the cattle, over all the earth and
over every creeping thing that creeps on the earth." Thus, in the

beginning, God assigned his authority over the whole creation to man, made in his image. The next use of the word *dominion* comes in verse 28, where God commands man to take charge of the creation: "Be fruitful and multiply; fill the earth and subdue it; have dominion over the fish of the sea, over the birds of the air, and over every living thing that moves on the earth." First, he commands creation to allow man to have dominion, then he commands man(kind) to have dominion.

You learn from the stories in Genesis that God delegates his authority not only to kings and leaders, but to all mankind. Mankind is created to be the head, or crown, of the creation. The dominion described here is the power of mankind over nature to manage livestock (animal husbandry, for example), and to change the landscape to meet their needs (construction of buildings, roads, dams, etc.). Dominion also means a person or group of people having power over people, as when a powerful enemy is strong enough to enslave, and when kings rule over nations. Governments (principalities and powers) also exercise dominion. The idea that all authority (dominion) comes from God has been recognized for many centuries, as shown by the idea of the divine right of kings. In business and military organizations, it has always been understood that authority can be delegated.

Words and works are the tools of dominion. God's commands are made by his word. By the Word all things were made (John 1:3). God said, "'Let there be light,' and there was light" (Gen. 1:3). Creation is the manifestation of God's Word, as you see in John 1:1-3: "In the beginning was the Word, and the Word was with God, and the Word was God. He was in the beginning with God. All things were made through Him, and without Him nothing was made that was made." He's speaking, of course, of Jesus. Not only mankind, but the whole of creation is made in God's image, for it is the manifestation of God—it is the visible, physical presentation of God's glory. Thus, in the beginning, God commanded creation to "let them have dominion". When God gave mankind dominion over creation, he gave them language to represent God's Word. His delegated authority and the inspiration of the spiritual connection was given to mankind in Genesis 2:7 when he breathed into man the breath of life. When a man (or woman) speaks, he (or she) is using the breath of God to command creation (watch what you say, for you will be held accountable for your words). According to verse 15, after God planted the garden in Eden, he put the man there to cultivate and keep it. Cultivate and keep are the works.

All went well for, probably, a day and a half (my guess). Then came the disconnect of sin, whereby the inspiration of faith and obedience were lost to mankind. God said because of their sin, the ground was cursed: "Cursed is the ground for your sake; In toil you shall eat of it All the days of your life. Both thorns and thistles it shall bring forth for you, And you shall eat the herb of the field. In the sweat of your face you shall eat bread Till you return to the ground, For out of it you were taken; For dust you are, And to dust you shall return." (Genesis 3: 17-19). Mankind still had dominion, because the gifts and calling of God are irrevocable (Romans 11:29). But they disconnected, by rebellion, from knowing the will of God, and now they were acting in accordance with their own will. They were trying to make it on their own authority. The results were disastrous. Acting with the full authority of God, but without being connected to his will, they began the downward spiral to destruction, as they began working in accordance with their own selfish desires. They killed each other, they built great cities, they established kingdoms, and they fought wars.

But God remains faithful and full of grace and mercy to those who seek his will. Those who seek his will are relatively few. Enoch and Noah found grace. Abraham, Isaac, Jacob, Joseph, Moses, Joshua, Caleb, Gideon, Samson, Samuel, Saul, David, Solomon, Elijah, Hezekiah, and many other prophets and kings, found grace. But unknown (except to God) myriads perished, and are perishing today, without grace because of a lack of guidance. God is the source of that guidance, but mankind cannot see it without the spiritual connection. God had to take action for man to be able to execute dominion in accordance with his will. He sent his Son, Jesus, to reestablish the spiritual connection that will allow God's will to be done on earth as it is in heaven. Jesus showed how to exercise dominion by the works he did on earth.

Jesus' first recorded miracle was to turn water into wine at the wedding feast in Capernaum. He cast out demons with a word, amazing people all over Judea with his power and authority. He said, "I must preach the kingdom of God to the other cities also, because for this purpose I have been sent," (Luke 4:43). In Luke's story of the forgiving and healing of a paralytic, he says: "Now it happened on a certain day, as He was teaching, that there were Pharisees and teachers of the law sitting by, who had come out of every town of Galilee, Judea, and Jerusalem. And the power of the Lord was present to heal them." (Luke 5:17). In Luke 7:11-17, the story is told of how Jesus raised a widow's son from death. All the works mentioned to this point relate to dominion over Satan's domain, and sickness and disease.

He also proclaims dominion over the law (after all, he is the King). A few days after the wedding feast in Capernaum, where he turned the water into wine, the Jewish Passover feast was celebrated in Jerusalem. Jesus took charge at the temple, driving out the cattle being sold, and overturning the money changers' tables. He taught with authority in the synagogues. In Luke 5:24 he says, "'But that you may know that the Son of Man has power on earth to forgive sins' –He said to the man who was paralyzed,

'I say to you, arise, take up your bed, and go to your house.'"
In the story told in Mark 2: 23-28, when the Pharisees accused
Jesus because he allowed his disciples to gather and eat grain as
they passed through the fields, Jesus told them, "The Sabbath was
made for man, and not man for the Sabbath. Therefore the Son
of Man is also Lord of the Sabbath." (vv. 27-28).

He exercised dominion over the forces of nature. On two
occasions he multiplied loaves and fishes to feed multitudes (e.g.,
Matthew 14:13-21 and Matthew 15:32-39). Luke 8:24 tells the
story of how he calmed the sea, "And they came to Him and
awoke Him, saying, 'Master, Master, we are perishing!' Then He
arose and rebuked the wind and the raging of the water. And they
ceased, and there was a calm." After feeding the five thousand, he
walked on the sea (John 6:19): "So when they had rowed about
three or four miles, they saw Jesus walking on the sea and drawing
near the boat; and they were afraid." In verse 21, he domineers
over space and time: "Then they willingly received Him into the
boat, and immediately the boat was at the land where they were
going." They went from being only about four miles out to being
at the opposite shore in the blink of an eye. Matthew (21:18-22)
tells the story of Jesus causing a fig tree to wither with a word:
"And seeing a fig tree by the road, He came to it and found
nothing on it but leaves, and said to it, 'Let no fruit grow on you
ever again.' Immediately the fig tree withered away." (v. 19).

All the works Jesus did while he was in the world, he did
as a man. He always referred to himself as the "Son of Man."
His works were done to show mankind how to live the life God
intended them to live. He showed them how to live the life of
obedience to God in the spirit of humility and servanthood to
mankind; and he showed them how to live the life of power and
authority as the representatives of God to the creation. He often
expressed disappointment when his disciples didn't have faith to

do the works he was doing. When he calmed the sea, because they had been fearful, he said, "Where is your faith?" (Luke 8:25). He expected his disciples to be doing the works he was doing. After seeing the fig tree wither, the disciples were amazed. Jesus told them, "Assuredly, I say to you, if you have faith and do not doubt, you will not only do what was done to the fig tree, but also if you say to this mountain, 'Be removed and be cast into the sea,' it will be done. And whatever things you ask in prayer, believing, you will receive." (Matthew 21:21-22).

It's important to understand that the works Jesus was doing were done in the will of God: "For I have come down from heaven, not to do My own will, but the will of Him who sent Me. This is the will of the Father who sent Me, that of all He has given Me I should lose nothing, but should raise it up at the last day. And this is the will of Him who sent Me, that everyone who sees the Son and believes in Him may have everlasting life; and I will raise him up at the last day." (John 6:38-40).

The best part of dominion, for mankind, is the ability to live free from sin. John says, "Behold what manner of love the Father has bestowed on us, that we should be called children of God! Therefore the world does not know us, because it did not know Him. Beloved, now we are children of God; and it has not yet been revealed what we shall be, but we know that when He is revealed, we shall be like Him, for we shall see Him as He is. And everyone who has this hope in Him purifies himself, just as He is pure. Whoever commits sin also commits lawlessness, and sin is lawlessness. And you know that He was manifested to take away our sins, and in Him there is no sin. Whoever abides in Him does not sin. Whoever sins has neither seen Him nor known Him." (1 John 3:1-6).

Because you have become joint heirs with Christ, you are now in the family of the Law-maker. The law can't have any power over you, but you have come (by your new nature) to love the commandment of your Heavenly Father through the grace of the Lord, Jesus. "For whatever is born of God overcomes the world. And this is the victory that has overcome the world—our faith. Who is he who overcomes the world, but he who believes that Jesus is the Son of God?" (1 John 5:4-5). Having been restored to dominion, you have the authority of God over creation, just as Jesus did. You, as the Church, have become the Body of Christ, and now have been restored to full authority and dominion over creation as you go about doing the works he has given you. John says in 1 John 4:4, "You are of God, little children, and have overcome them, because He who is in you is greater than he who is in the world." As a man, Jesus was demonstrating to fallen mankind how they should be walking. He said he was always doing the will of his Father. "I can of Myself do nothing. As I hear, I judge; and My judgment is righteous, because I do not seek My own will but the will of the Father who sent Me." (John 5:30).

In his book, *Like a Mighty Wind*, Mel Tari, from Indonesia, tells of a great revival in that country during the 1970's. He and the gospel team he was a part of were involved in great miracles. The works included walking on water, changing water to wine, multiplying food, casting out demons, healing the sick, even raising the dead. This is faith and works acting together to produce dominion in modern times. This is the fulfillment of Jesus' promise in Mark 16:17-18, 20: "He who believes and is baptized will be saved; but he who does not believe will be condemned. And these signs will follow those who believe: In My name they will cast out demons; they will speak with new tongues; they will take up serpents; and if they drink anything deadly, it will by no means hurt them; they will lay hands on the sick, and they will recover." (v. 20): "And they went out and preached everywhere, the Lord working with them and confirming the word through the accompanying signs."

In Matthew 16:19, Jesus says to Peter, "And I will give you the keys of the kingdom of heaven, and whatever you bind on earth will be bound in heaven, and whatever you loose on earth will be loosed in heaven." This verse is the reason there are so many jokes about meeting Peter at the pearly gates. It has been interpreted to mean that Peter is the keeper of the keys of the kingdom of heaven. That is not the case. Jesus is the keeper of the keys to the kingdom of heaven, and he gives them to whomever he wants to give them. Jesus is no respecter of persons. If he gives the keys to Peter, he will just as surely give the keys to you. He intends for every believer to walk in his authority, so that whatever any believer binds on earth is bound in heaven, and whatever any believer may loose on earth is loosed in heaven. He has delegated authority not only to Peter, but to the entire Body of Christ, the Church.

You, the Church, as the Body of Christ, are expected to be doing the work of Jesus on earth (as it is in heaven). He has called you to do his work, according to his will. You can't be doing all the works that Jesus did all the time. On the other hand, don't expect to be limited by time and space or any physical obstacles when it comes time to do the work Jesus gives you. The only limit you need to be concerned about is the failure to be inspired. Jesus gives you authority to do the work through the inspiration and power of the Holy Spirit. You see in the story of the healing of the paralytic, "And the power of the Lord was present to heal them." (Luke 5:17). This text shows, first, that the power of the Lord to heal may not have been with him at all times. At least for this occasion it was especially powerful. Second, it shows that he was using the *power of the Lord* for the healing miracles. The source of that power is the Holy Spirit, given by God the Father. John says,

"For whatever is born of God overcomes the world. And this is the victory that has overcome the world—our (your) faith. Who is he who overcomes the world, but he who believes that Jesus is the Son of God? This is He who came by water and blood—Jesus Christ; not only by water, but by water and blood. And it is the Spirit who bears witness, because the Spirit is truth. For there are three that bear witness in heaven: the Father, the Word, and the Holy Spirit; and these three are one." (1 John 5:4-8). The heavenly witness is intended to be carried out in the world by the Body of Christ, the Church.

One night, a few weeks after being born again, as I lay in bed, praising and worshiping Jesus, prior to going to sleep, I felt the presence of Jesus come to stand at the foot of my bed. From him came the purest love, like an electric current, that flowed from him, into my toes, through my body, and out the top of my head to God the Father, and from there, back to Jesus. I was given to understand that this current of purest love flowing through me was God, the Holy Spirit. I knew, too, that this was the Trinity of God. The Three-in-One, Father, Son, and Holy Spirit, and, most exciting of all, he was including me in that unity, for the Holy Spirit flowing through me, bound him to me and me to him. I immediately knew that this was the baptism in the Holy Spirit I had been reading about and praying for. I also knew that this is how unity is achieved in the Body of Christ. The Spirit now flowing through me, binds me together with Father, Son and Holy Spirit, and is also flowing through all born-again, Spirit-filled Christians.

This is the unity Jesus was talking about when he prayed in John 17:20-23: "I do not pray for these alone [meaning the disciples], but also for those who will believe in Me through their word; that they all may be one, as You, Father, are in Me, and I in You; that they also may be one in Us, that the world may believe that You sent Me. And the glory which You gave Me I have given them, that they may be one just as We are one; I in them and You in me; that they may be made perfect in one, and that the world may know that you have sent Me, and have loved them as You have loved Me." As the pure love of God was flowing through me, I thought, "If this keeps up, I'll be transported directly to heaven." Then I thought, "This is the baptism in the Holy Spirit. Now I'll be able to heal the sick". Immediately upon thinking this thought, the love flow stopped and I felt the presence of God leave (of course, the presence of God never leaves, he just stopped the experience I was having). I later came to understand that he stopped the experience because of the error of my thinking. It is impossible that I will ever heal the sick. It is impossible for any human to heal the sick. All healing (and all power, dominion and authority) comes from God the Father, through Jesus, the Son, by the power of the Holy Spirit, on earth, as it is in heaven.

Don't expect to exercise authority over everything just because you have the authority of Jesus. You have all authority because you belong to Jesus, but you are not omnipotent and omnipresent, as Jesus is. You aren't going to walk on the water and turn water into wine on a whim just because you are a Christian. For such work you must have the full authority of God, which comes by faith. According to Hebrews 11:1, "faith is the substance (realization) of things hoped for, the evidence (confidence) of things not seen." Verse 3 says, "By faith we understand that the worlds were framed by the word of God, so that the things which are seen were not made of things which are visible." Psalm 127:1 says, "Unless the Lord builds the house, They labor in vain who build it; Unless the Lord guards the city, The watchman stays awake in vain."

Paul says (Romans 10:17), "So then faith comes by hearing, and hearing by the word of God." Faith is a spiritual gift (1 Corinthians 12:9). 1 John 5:14-15 says, "Now this is the confidence that we have in Him, that if we ask anything according to His will, He hears us. And if we know that He hears us, whatever we ask, we know that we have the petitions that we have asked of Him." How do you know you are asking according to his will? He gives understanding. See 1 John 5:20: "And we know that the Son of God has come and has given us an understanding, that we may know Him who is true; and we are in Him who is true, in His Son Jesus Christ." The scope of your work is limited to the degree you are inspired. Your inspiration comes from Jesus, through the Holy Spirit. Inspiration is closely linked to faith (maybe inspiration is faith). You get inspired while abiding in Christ, sometimes by prayer and fasting, other times simply by knowing you are walking in his will.

John also tells how to know you are walking in his will in 1 John 2:3-6: "Now by this we know that we know Him, if we keep His commandments. He who says, 'I know Him,' and does not keep His commandments, is a liar, and the truth is not in him. But whoever keeps His word, truly the love of God is perfected in him. By this we know that we are in Him. He who says he abides in Him ought himself also to walk just as He walked." Jesus explains about this abiding in the gospel of John, chapter 15 (John 15:1-17):

> 1) "I am the true vine, and My Father is the vinedresser. 2) Every branch in Me that does not bear fruit He takes away; and every branch that bears fruit He prunes, that it may bear more fruit. 3) You are already clean because of the word which I have spoken to you [faith comes by hearing]. 4) Abide in Me, and I in you. As the branch cannot bear fruit of itself, unless it abides in the vine, neither can you, unless you abide in Me. 5) I am the vine, you are the branches. He who abides in Me, and I in him, bears much fruit;

for without Me you can do nothing. 6) If anyone does not abide in Me, he is cast out as a branch and is withered; and they gather them and throw them into the fire, and they are burned. 7) If you abide in Me, and My words abide in you, you will ask what you desire, and it shall be done for you. 8) By this My Father is glorified, that you bear much fruit; so you will be My disciples. 9) As the Father loved Me, I also have loved you; abide in My love. 10) If you keep My commandments, you will abide in My love, just as I have kept My Father's commandments and abide in His love. 11) These things I have spoken to you, that My joy may remain in you, and that your joy may be full. 12) This is My commandment, that you love one another as I have loved you. 13) Greater love has no one than this, than to lay down one's life for his friends. 14) You are My friends if you do whatever I command you. 15) No longer do I call you servants, for a servant does not know what his Master is doing; but I have called you friends, for all things that I heard from My Father I have made known to you. 16) You did not choose Me, but I chose you and appointed you that you should go and bear fruit, and that your fruit should remain, that whatever you ask the Father in My name He may give you. 17) These things I command you, that you love one another."

You can study this passage for a lifetime and continue to get more and more out of it. You know you are abiding in his will if you have peace, love, and joy in your walk. In Matthew 11:29-30, he says, "Take my yoke upon you and learn from Me, for I am gentle (meek) and lowly in heart, and you will find rest for your souls. For My yoke is easy and My burden is light." His yoke is more than light. It is buoyant. It lifts you up and makes you full of joy. If you do not have joy and peace in your walk, you need to get back to prayer and fasting. If you are ministering in love, you know you are abiding in Jesus. Love flows (by the Holy Spirit) through the Vine (Jesus), and you are the branch. That's why James can say (James 1:2): "My brethren, count it all joy when you fall into various trials". Your fruit is meant to be picked and consumed. It is the destiny of fruit to be used up by passing fruit gatherers. Some will abuse it. Others will receive it with joy. This is where "The Parable of the Sower"'" applies (read Matthew 13:1-9).

As the branch it is your duty (destiny) to abide in the Vine, allowing him to produce fruit through you until you are used up. At the end of your productive life, the Master Gardener will prune you to make room for new growth, and you will join Jesus in his eternal glory. According to Psalm 73:24: "You will guide me with your counsel, And afterward, receive me to glory." It's what Jesus himself did. He came to show the way, to set the pattern, then submitted himself to be killed on our behalf. He said, "Remember the word that I said to you, 'A servant is not greater than his master.' If they persecuted Me, they will also persecute you. If they kept My word they will keep yours also". (John 15:20).

John says in 1 John 3:13-23: 13) "Do not marvel, my brethren if the world hates you. 14) We know that we have passed from death to life, because we love the brethren. He who does not love his brother abides in death. 15) Whoever hates his brother is a murderer, and you know that no murderer has eternal life abiding in him. 16) By this we know love, because He laid down His life for us. And we also ought to lay down our lives for the brethren. 17) But whoever has this world's goods, and sees his brother in need, and shuts up his heart from him, how does the love of God abide in him? 18) My little children, let us not love in word or in tongue, but in deed and in truth. 19) And by this we know that we are of the truth, and shall assure our hearts before Him. 20)

For if our heart condemns us, God is greater than our heart, and knows all things. 21) Beloved, if our heart does not condemn us, we have confidence toward God. 22) And whatever we ask we receive from Him, because we keep His commandments and do those things that are pleasing in His sight. 23) And this is His commandment: that we should believe on the name of His Son Jesus Christ and love one another, as He gave us commandment. Now he who keeps His commandments abides in Him, and He in him. And by this we know that He abides in us, by the Spirit whom He has given us."

The ultimate dominion is found in this—that you follow in the footsteps of the King of kings. In John 16:13-15 he says, "However, when He, the Spirit of truth, has come, He will guide you into all truth; for He will not speak on His own authority, but whatever He hears He will speak; and He will tell you things to come. He will glorify Me, for He will take of what is Mine and declare it to you. All things that the Father has are Mine. Therefore I said that He will take of Mine and declare it to you." I say with Jude (24-25): "Now to Him who is able to keep you from stumbling, And to present you faultless Before the presence of His glory with exceeding joy, To God our Savior, Who alone is wise, Be glory and majesty, Dominion and power, Both now and forever. Amen." Get the gift of the Holy Spirit. Hear his voice. Obey his word. Do his work. As you abide in the Vine, all his power and authority will go with you.

Abortion

Abortion is unmitigated, premeditated murder, in the first degree. It is perpetrated by selfish, immoral, ruthless parents and greedy abortion clinicians who are guilty of the blood of innocent babies. These babies have a God-given right to life, and are robbed of it without being given the right to defend themselves. There can never be any justification for killing the innocent child. The only way abortion can be justified is if the action would be redefined to mean saving the baby alive and killing the father and mother. The baby is innocent, never having done anything worthy of death. The parents are guilty of selfish, immoral and ruthless behavior worthy of death. Politicians who promote the right to legalized abortion and the people who vote for them are aiding and abetting murder and are guilty as accessories before the fact.

Because of the shed blood of innocent babies, the land is under a curse. Except by the prayers of the saints, the land cannot receive rain for watering. Instead, the rain (and snow) can only come with disastrous torrential downpours with damaging winds accompanying. Flooding, hurricanes, tornadoes and deadly blizzards will continue to be the norm until the killing stops, and for several years (probably seven) following, until the land is cleansed of the innocent blood. It is possible, if the people would repent from committing abortions, mourn the loss of the innocent babies, and raise a memorial monument in their memory, the Lord may be entreated to remove the curse. I think it is unlikely the people will repent.

Have you thanked your mother for not aborting you?

Words Precious Beyond Measure

The words of life from the kingdom of God are precious beyond measure. One may rarely come upon them as if by accident (there are no accidents in the kingdom of God), but it is the norm to find them only by diligently seeking. In the spring or early summer of 1973, when I first met Jesus, I was very eager to share my new-found joy. As I was driving home from work one day, a man signaled to me from the side of the road that he wanted a ride. I had already decided that I would take every opportunity to share the gospel with as many people as I could. I decided, when I could, I would pick up hitchhikers and let them know they were being given a ride in the name of Jesus and because of his love. The man I was about to meet wore dirty, ragged clothes, and had dirty, ragged hair, mustache and beard. He appeared to be in his late thirties. As he got into the car, it became apparent that he was even smellier than he was dirty and ragged. He stunk of sweat, urine, and alcohol. He thanked me profusely with halitosis to knock my socks off. I profusely and, I thought, modestly, responded with, "You shouldn't be thanking me, you should be thanking Jesus. It's because of him that I decided to pick you up."

He began telling me what a fine, upstanding Christian he had always been, and that he even knew a preacher once, and that, for sure, he didn't need anyone to be telling *him* about Jesus. He kept going on, for the whole trip, about how good he had always been and what a great Christian life he had always lived. I never had a chance to tell him what he needed to do to receive Jesus. By the time I dropped him off, I was sorry I had even tried to offer him my precious words of life and witness. After I left him, I agonized half a day over why I was not able to bring a witness to the man. Then the Lord reminded me of the scripture at Matthew 7:6 (KJV): "Give not that which is holy unto the dogs, neither cast ye your pearls before swine, lest they trample them under their feet, and turn again and rend you." Well, I can tell you that I certainly felt that man had trampled my holy intentions under foot. I am grateful that he didn't turn and rend me. I made up my mind to be more careful about how I went about sharing the gospel from then on.

Because of this incident, I began to wait carefully upon the Lord to show me opportunities to share. One day a colleague at work mentioned that he admired my Christian walk because I didn't "flaunt" my religion or push it off on anyone. I responded by telling him that the Lord has told us not to cast our pearls before swine. Afterwards he became contrary, even hostile toward me. I asked another colleague for an explanation of his attitude toward me, and he explained that he (first colleague) thought I had been referring to him personally as swine when I told him why I wasn't pushy with my religion. The injured party remained aloof from me from then on. I never got a chance to talk to him further, or to share with him my true love for him, or to tell him the true meaning of the Lord's command.

I tell these stories to illustrate how carefully we must guard the precious words of life in the kingdom of God. Every word from the Lord is a precious gem, eternal in truth, and infinite in scope. When we are born again Christians, we have become the Body of Christ to the world, and our words are God's Word. The whole world watches our actions and listens to our words to try to trap us and to say, "See the evil in this person who claims to be a Christian." This is the way the Scribes and Pharisees treated Jesus when he was in the world, and we continue in the world in his Name.

The Prospector

The kingdom of God is like a man prospecting for gold. He has abandoned the idea that gold will magically appear at his doorstep, and he has determined that he must go searching for it. First he studies diligently to learn how to find and mine it. Then he sells all his possessions to buy equipment and supplies for the quest, says goodbye to family and friends, and heads out into the wilderness alone to seek his treasure. When he finds the mother lode, he digs out the ore and refines it until he has as much fine gold as he can carry. Then he takes his treasure home to family and friends to share his good fortune.

The Cowboy Hat

A cowboy must have three hats:

White: for courtin' and Sunday-go-to-meetin'.

Black: for barn dancin' and Saturday night carousin'.

Brown: for work. Brown is for work because, if it falls off into the corral water, all the cowboy has to do is rinse it off in the horse trough and nobody can tell the difference. If a black or white hat falls into the corral water, the stain is too noticeable.

Regardless of the color, it must hold enough water to give his horse a drink.

Pocket Knife Rules

Safety first (last and always):

Opening: Grip the handle firmly between thumb and forefinger, blade side up, in the left hand (if you are right-handed). Be sure fingers are below the top edge of the handle. For the selected blade, be sure the opening motion will carry the tip of the blade away from your hand. To start the opening process, it is usually necessary to insert the thumbnail of the right hand into the groove provided. As soon as the blade is open enough, grasp the blade firmly between the thumb and forefinger and continue the opening motion until the blade locks into the fully open position. If the locking mechanism isn't working or the knife doesn't have a locking mechanism, throw the knife away and get one that locks safely.

Closing: Grip the handle firmly between thumb and forefinger, cutting edge up, in the left hand. Be sure fingers are below the top edge of the handle. Grasp the blade firmly between the thumb and forefinger and fold the blade into the closed position. Sometimes the locking mechanism will be strong enough that the blade cannot be started with this method. When this is the case, throw the knife away and get one that can be closed by this method.

Cutting: The knife is for cutting only! Never use it as a screwdriver or for prying on anything. Failure to follow this rule will *always* result in damage to the blade. Always cut with the sharp edge moving away from all parts of your body. Do not use much force for cutting. If cutting requires a lot of force, either the blade needs to be honed, or the material is too hard for the knife. If you are using a folding knife for whittling or carving, it is safer to use softer woods such as pine and poplar. For harder woods, wood carving tools and fixed-blade knives should be used.

Never lay it down except in its designated place at home.

Keep your knife at home in the same place all the time. Never take it anyplace with you except when you know you will have a need for it. When it is necessary to carry it with you, be sure it is in a secure pocket deep enough that the knife will not fall out as you move about. Put nothing else in the pocket with the knife. That way, it will not come out accidently when you intend to take something else out. When you have a need to use it, take it out of your pocket, use it, then immediately return it to your pocket. Never lay it down! As soon as you get home and have no more need for it, return it to its designated place.

Printed in the United States
By Bookmasters